WOW!
I didn't know that
SURPRISING FACTS ABOUT THE HUMAN BODY

You think 70,000 thoughts a day.

KINGFISHER
LONDON & NEW YORK

Copyright © Kingfisher 2014
Published in the United States by Kingfisher,
175 Fifth Ave., New York, NY 10010
Kingfisher is an imprint of Macmillan Children's Books, London.
All rights reserved.

Distributed in the U.S. and Canada by Macmillan, 175 Fifth Ave., New York, NY 10010

Library of Congress Cataloging-in-Publication data has been applied for.

Author: Emma Dods
Design and styling: Amy McSimpson
Cover design: Mike Davis
Illustrations: Marc Aspinall
Consultant: Dr. Patricia Macnair

ISBN: 978-0-7534-7118-0 (HC)
ISBN: 978-0-7534-7185-2 (PB)

Kingfisher books are available for special promotions and premiums.
For details contact: Special Markets Department, Macmillan, 175 Fifth Ave., New York, NY 10010.

For more information, please visit www.kingfisherbooks.com

Printed in China
1 3 5 7 9 8 6 4 2
1TR/1113/WKT/UG/140WF

WOW!
I didn't know that
HUMAN BODY

You use 20 muscles when you smile.

Every person has a unique tongue print.

Your thumb is the same length as your nose.

KINGFISHER

NEW YORK

Our bodies are mostly made of water. Newborn babies are almost 80 percent water, while adults are only about 55 to 60 percent water.

You have enough carbon in your body to fill the middle of 900 pencils.

Our bodies are made of tiny amounts of many different chemicals. An adult's body has enough iron to make a nail that is 3 inches (7cm) long.

4

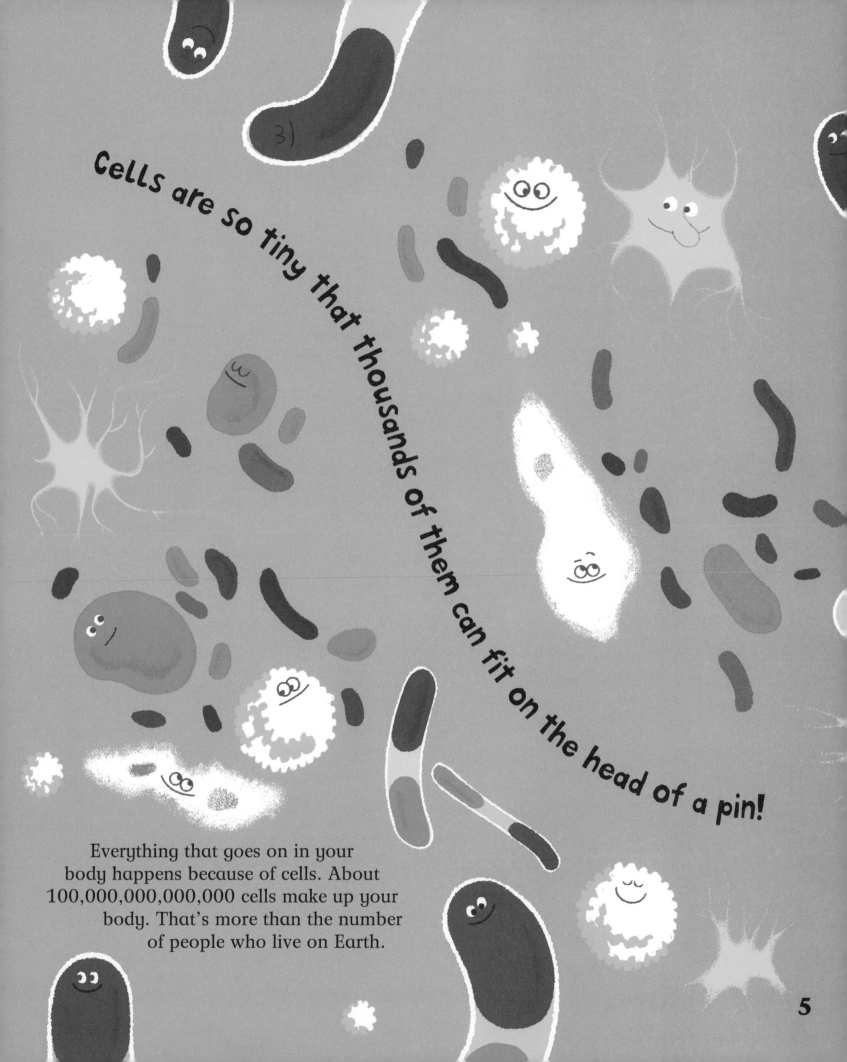

Cells are so tiny that thousands of them can fit on the head of a pin!

Everything that goes on in your body happens because of cells. About 100,000,000,000,000 cells make up your body. That's more than the number of people who live on Earth.

Your nose and ears never ever stop growing.

The chemical substance that makes you grow is made by your brain when you are fast asleep.

You are about 0.4 inches (1cm) taller in the morning than in the evening.

The length of your foot is the same as the distance between your wrist and the inside of your elbow. Go on—try it!

Fingernails grow three times faster than toenails, and the nails on the hand you write with grow the fastest of all.

The older you get, the slower your fingernails grow.

Hair grows about 0.4 inches (1cm) every month, so it might take three or four years to grow your hair all the way down your back.

Children grow faster in the spring and the summer.

Hair we go to more body facts . . . .

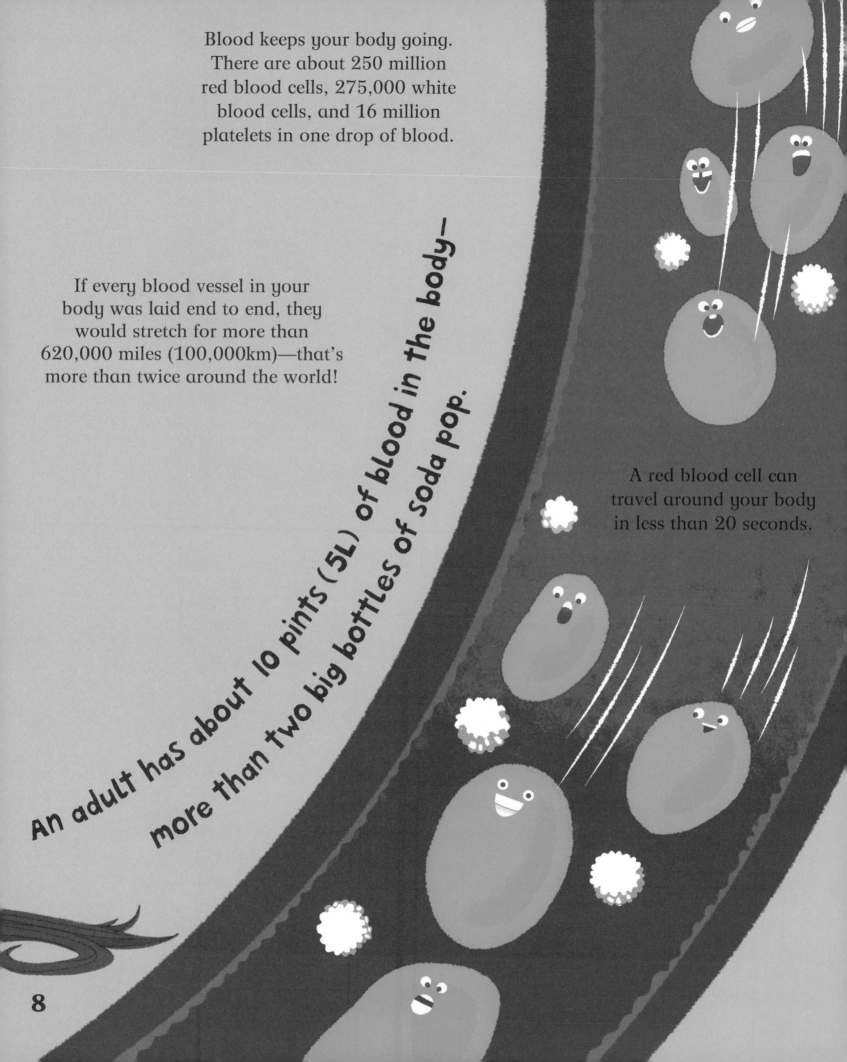

Blood keeps your body going. There are about 250 million red blood cells, 275,000 white blood cells, and 16 million platelets in one drop of blood.

If every blood vessel in your body was laid end to end, they would stretch for more than 620,000 miles (100,000km)—that's more than twice around the world!

An adult has about 10 pints (5L) of blood in the body— more than two big bottles of soda pop.

A red blood cell can travel around your body in less than 20 seconds.

If you give a tennis ball a hard squeeze, you're using about the same amount of force that your heart uses to pump blood around your body.

Your heart grows as you grow. You can't see your heart, but it is the same size as your fist! An adult's heart is the size of both of your fists held together.

Even when it is resting, the muscles of your heart are working twice as hard as the leg muscles of a person sprinting.

An adult's heart beats more than 100,000 times every day, and yours beats more than 150,000 times every day.

Your heart will beat about three billion times during your lifetime!

who has jumped rope today?

9

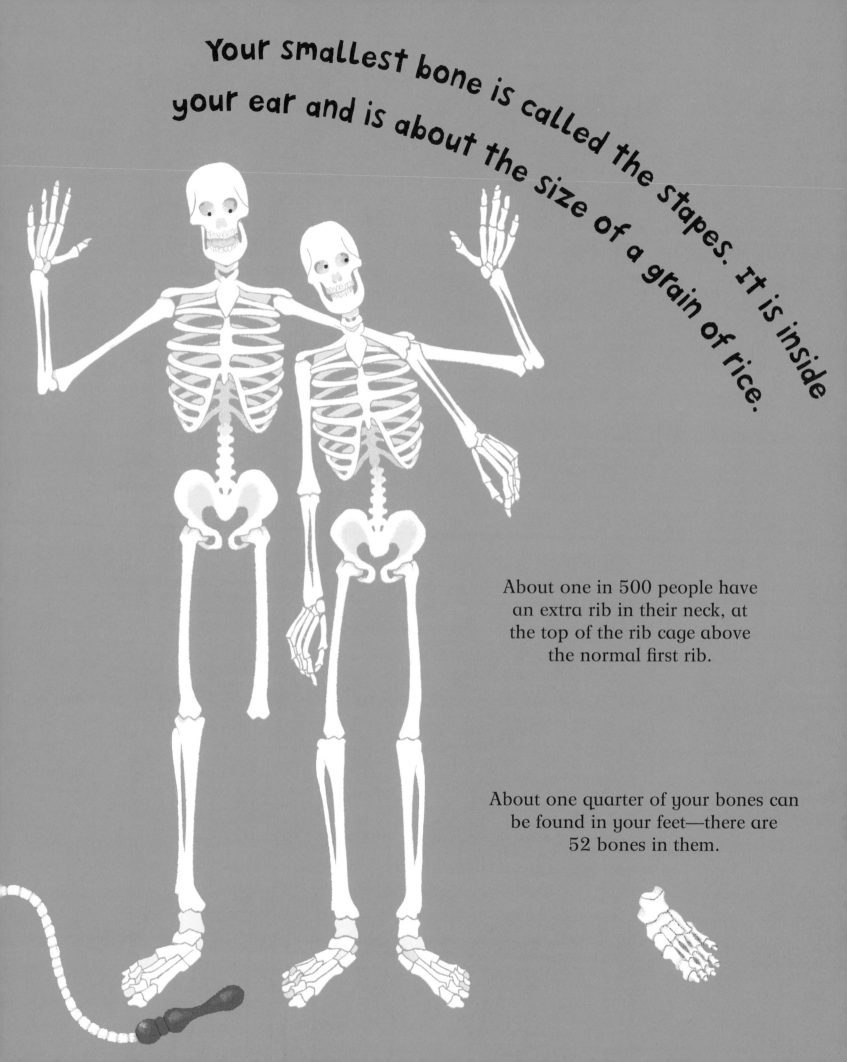

Your smallest bone is called the stapes. It is inside your ear and is about the size of a grain of rice.

About one in 500 people have an extra rib in their neck, at the top of the rib cage above the normal first rib.

About one quarter of your bones can be found in your feet—there are 52 bones in them.

Babies are born with 300 to 350 bones. As we grow up, we end up with only 206 bones. Many small bones fuse together to make the skeleton stronger.

Humans have a kind of tail. Four tiny bones are joined together at the bottom of the spine to form the tailbone.

EEEEEEK!

A broken bone can mend itself. A broken arm can take six weeks or more to heal, and a broken leg can take up to 12 weeks. The broken bone is wrapped in a cast.

A mouse has more bones than an adult human.

More than half of your body is made from muscles. Their main job is to move the body. They also support the skeleton and keep our shape or posture.

There are more than 650 named muscles in the human body.

Your largest muscle is the gluteus maximus

Woof! Woof!

Your smallest muscle, the stapedius, is hidden in your ear. It is about 0.04 inches (1mm) long.

Your fingers don't have muscles. Instead, they have tendons—stringlike structures attached to muscles higher up in your arm. These move your fingers in the same way that a puppeteer moves a puppet on strings.

FINISH

Whoops!

It is in your bottom.

Before their second birthday, the average baby will have used their muscles to crawl and walk about 93 miles (150km).

13

Your brain looks like a giant, wrinkled walnut. It controls your entire body.

More of your brain is devoted to controlling your hands than any other part of your body.

An elephant's brain is about four times larger than a human's brain.

Your brain is busier during the night than during the day.

An adult human brain weighs about three times more than a chimpanzee's brain, nearly 50 times more than a cat's brain, and about 700 times more than a rat's brain.

14

Your brain uses the same amount of power as a lightbulb.

It is impossible to tickle yourself because your brain knows what is coming and ignores the "tickle."

Hehehe! Giggle! Giggle!

The brain does not have sensory nerve endings and so does not feel pain. This means that surgeons can operate on the brain while a person is awake.

15

No one smells the same. This is because of the billions of friendly bacteria that live on our skin.

Every 28 days, you lose your entire outer layer of skin. In the time it takes you to read this page, you have probably lost around 30,000 to 40,000 dead skin cells. That's about 9 pounds (4kg) of cells every year (about the weight of a cat)!

No one has the same pattern of fingerprint. Even identical twins have different fingerprints.

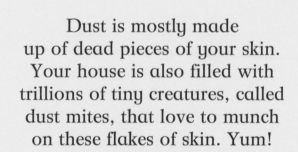

Dust is mostly made up of dead pieces of your skin. Your house is also filled with trillions of tiny creatures, called dust mites, that love to munch on these flakes of skin. Yum!

16

You have as many hairs as a chimpanzee. However, your hairs are much thinner over most of your body.

Blond-haired people have more hairs on their head than dark-haired people.

In your lifetime, you will grow about 6 feet (1.8m) of nose hair. That's more than the height of most adults!

Skin can feel pain, cold, pressure, heat, and vibrations.

The first sense you get is touch. You have this sense before you are born!

Dogs can pick up more than 40 times more smells than humans can. The bigger the dog's nose, the better its sense of smell. That's why bloodhounds make the best tracking dogs.

After the age of 60, the senses of smell and taste decline.

Our sense of taste is actually mostly smell. Try eating and holding your nose—can you taste properly?

Butterflies taste with their feet.

Our noses can recognize more than 10,000 different smells!

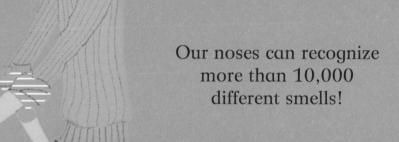

who is hopping away from the picnic?

19

Your eyes simply collect light signals—it's your brain that decides what you are seeing.

Some people's senses are mixed up . . . For example, they can taste certain foods when they read words or see color when they hear some sounds.

We can't see behind us without turning our head, but rabbits and parrots can! That's because their eyes are on the sides of their head.

Squawk!

Animals are better at hearing than we are. Fireworks sound more than five times louder to cats and dogs.

Sailors once thought that wearing an earring would improve their eyesight.

Ears don't just help you hear, they also help you balance.

Your eyes can take in more information than the world's largest telescope.

We blink about 20,000 times every day.

You can see the difference between almost one million different colors.

What is that smell?

21

The acid in your stomach is so strong, it can dissolve metal.

Cows release about 420 pints (200L) of gas every day.

Most people fart up to 25 times a day—that's about 4 pints (2L) of gas!

It takes more than a day for food to go in one end and out the other.

You will spend about three years of your life on the toilet.

Beans, cabbage, artichokes, lentils, prunes, apples, and Brussels sprouts all make you fart more!

Astronauts are the reason we know so much about burping and farting. NASA scientists were worried that a burp or fart in space might cause an explosion . . . so they did a lot of research on people's gas!

When astronauts come back from space, they can be up to 2 inches (5cm) taller.

A burp in space is a " wet burp." Gas comes out of the nose and mouth . . . along with the contents of the stomach. Eeew!

Whose tail is this?

Most people take seven minutes to fall asleep.

Teenagers need as much sleep as small children (about ten hours), while those over 65 need the least of all (about six hours).

Hooo! Hooo!

Snoring can be as loud as a jackhammer.

In your lifetime, you will sleep for a little more than 25 years.

24

Many people sleepwalk, but some even draw amazing pictures cook, or write e-mails in their sleep!

Some people can take naps with their eyes open, having quick sleeps without even being aware of it.

The longest anyone has gone without any sleep is 18 days, 21 hours, and 40 minutes, during a rocking chair marathon.

who has walked away?

sob, sob

We can still survive if we lose some organs, from a kidney to a lung, our tonsils, appendix, and even the large intestine.

It's not unusual to have an extra organ— a third kidney or an extra finger!

26

If you were able to spread out all the surfaces inside your lungs, they would cover an entire tennis court.

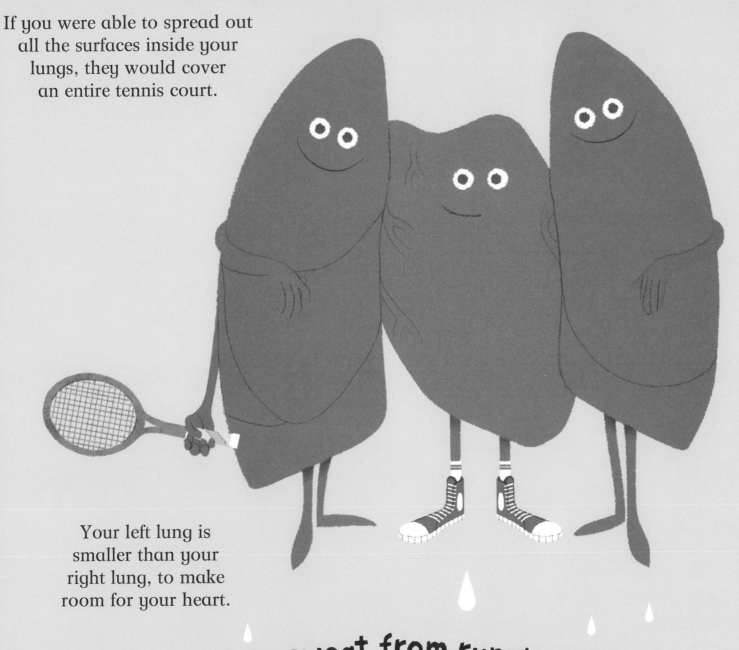

Your left lung is smaller than your right lung, to make room for your heart.

Our eyebrows keep sweat from running into our eyes!

27

The ancient Romans used pee as a mouthwash, to kill bacteria.

Ancient Romans used pigeon droppings to lighten their hair!

SPLAT!

Ancient Romans thought that broken ribs could be healed by applying a mixture of goat's poop and wine.

Vikings used urine to start fires.

False teeth were first made by the Etruscans, in the 600s B.C.

Egyptian pharaohs had people who were official bottom wipers.

Hippocrates, an ancient Greek doctor, took samples of vomit, snot, earwax, and pee. He then tasted each one (or would get the patient to) to try to figure out why the patient was sick.

What has made someone throw up?

Ancient Egyptians shaved off their eyebrows to mourn the death of their cats.

Ancient Egyptians mixed together salt, mint, dried iris flower, and pepper for their toothpaste.

Ancient Egyptian dentists suggested putting a dead, hot mouse in your mouth to cure bad breath!

Ewww!

We all have billions of tiny animals harmlessly roaming around our bodies—from tiny mites living in our eyelashes, to billions of friendly bacteria in our intestines.

You have more sweat glands in your feet than anywhere else—about one quarter of a million of them. Bacteria on the skin like to use this oily sweat for food, breaking it down to produce smelly gas.

If your feet didn't sweat, you wouldn't be able to play soccer, dance, or do anything else that involved walking or running. Sweating keeps the skin on your feet soft and flexible.

Earwax can be yellow, orange, gray, green, or brown!

The longest recorded sneezing fit lasted for 978 days.

AaaaaaaCHOO!

A cough zooms out at 62 miles (100km) per hour!

A sneeze can blast out at 103 miles (166km) per hour!

It is possible to sneeze with your eyes open.

Your nose makes about 2.5 to 3 cups (600 to 700ml) of snot each day—that's about two cans of soda pop.

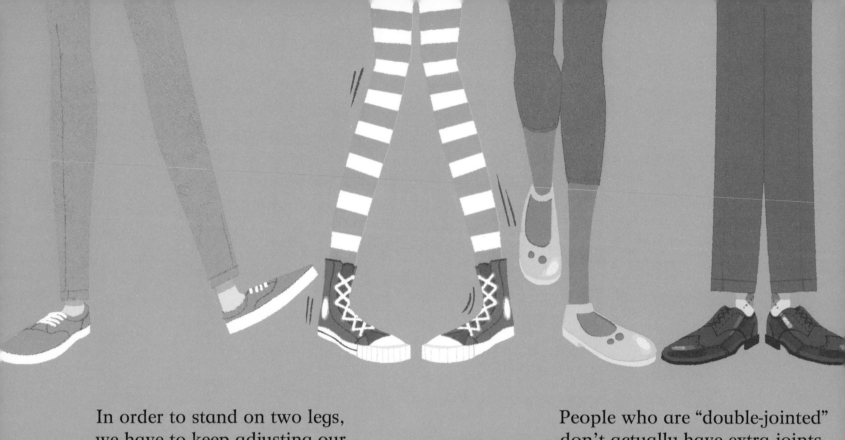

In order to stand on two legs, we have to keep adjusting our posture or we will fall over.

People who are "double-jointed" don't actually have extra joints, but they have very loose joints that allow their bodies to twist and bend.

You use 300 muscles just to stand still.

Balancing on only one leg is very difficult. The record of 76 hours and 40 minutes for standing on one leg, set in 1997 by Arulanantham Suresh Joachim in Sri Lanka, is amazing!